Yesterday and Today:
Going to School

Phylliss Adams

DOMINIE PRESS
Pearson Learning Group

ISBN 0-7685-0588-7

Printed in Singapore

4 5 6 7 8 07 06

Dominie
Press
Pearson Learning Group

1-800-321-3106
www.pearsonlearning.com

Table of Contents

Today was a special day
at our school.

It was Grandparents' Day.

Our grandparents came to
school with us.

We showed our grandparents our classroom.

We showed our grandparents our books.

We told our grandparents what we did at school.

8

Our grandparents showed us old photographs of *their* school.

Our grandparents told us what *they* did at school when *they* were children.

"In the old days, I went to a small school in the country," said Grandpa Gomez.

"The school only had three classrooms. We each sat at our own desk. The desks were in straight rows."

"Our old school didn't have a library. A bookmobile came to our school each week. We got library books from the bookmobile."

"I went to a big school in the city," said Grandma Sims.

"Each morning, we read stories from big, fat reading books. Sometimes we saw a film," she said.

"Sometimes we sang along with a record," said Grandma Sims.

"We all loved singing songs."

"We all love singing songs, too!" we said.

We all sang together.

"Just like in the old days!"
said our grandparents.

"Just like today!" we said.

Picture Glossary

bookmobile:

photographs:

grandparents:

Index